GRANDMOTHERS
A TO W, Y AND Z

A Book of
Multicultural Poems
About Grandmothers

Guda Gayle-Evans

Published by True Beginnings Publishing. Copyright by Guda Gayle-Evans, 2023.

ISBN-13: 978-1-947082-32-8

This book is a compilation of poetry to represent the role of grandmothers and how they affect their grandchildren's lives. All poetry is presented as a whole by the Author, included donated pieces. Herein, the poetry is not meant to contain every aspect of every culture and is presented as an artistic representation of grandmothers from each culture researched by the Author.

Dedication

This work is dedicated to the memory of my parents Charles and Leanora Gayle who were the best parents and grandparents and to all the wonderful women and men who have so gladly embraced the role of grandparent.

Table of Contents

Dedication

Introduction

Who is a grandmother? A grandmother is the mother of either of one's parent. Therefore, everyone has two biological grandmothers. The father's mother is one's *paternal* grandmother, while the mother's mother is one's *maternal* grandmother.

There is no specific age at which one becomes a grandmother. It is culturally defined. In the United States, for example, 43% of the population become grandparents in their fifties, while 37% become grandparents in their forties. The average age for becoming a grandmother, in the United States, is 48 years (2010 Statistics). In many other cultures, the age at which one becomes a grandmother tends to be older. There is also a diversity of names for grandmothers. This too is based on culture (Appendix B) and interestingly, there is even a diversity of names for grandmothers within a particular culture.

The role of the grandmother is also diverse, culturally defined and, in some cultures, the grandmother's role may be non-specific. In many Western cultures, for example, the grandmother is the nurturer to her grandchildren and provide assistance with childcare, if this becomes necessary. She may also be the one to whom relatives go for advice because she has life experience, as well as experience in having and raising children. However, these are not required roles.

In some other cultures, however, the role of the grandmother may be more specific. In Liberian-American culture, for example, the grandmother is seen as the "cornerstone" of the family unit and shares in decision-making, as well as financial responsibilities. In Chinese culture, where the kinship role is highly regarded, mothers and their daughters are expected to ensure the family stays connected. Grandmothers are expected to be actively engaged with their grandchildren. They are actually expected to participate in the raising of their grandchildren.

In many Native American cultures, the grandmother's role is also specific. Although there are over five hundred Native American tribes in the United States, all with different attributes, they share many similarities. Native American cultures tend to operate as communities and clans. Respect and reverence among families, tribes, and clans are highly important values. However, a well-established role of grandmothers, in many of these communities, is their contribution to the culture. They are responsible for taking care of, as well as raising, their grandchildren. Although sometimes it is because of necessity, it is mostly an expectation. In these communities, a vital role of the grandmother is providing guidance and transmitting cultural values to their grandchildren. As in many other cultures, the grandmother in these communities is also seen as a source of wisdom due to lived experience (Gayle-Evans, 2022).

Japanese grandmothers are also expected to keep the family together. They are considered "kin-keepers." They are responsible for taking care of their grandchildren on a daily basis. Unlike some cultures where co-parenting is voluntary, they are expected to co-parent and, like many Native American communities, they are expected to teach their children Japanese cultural values and traditions (Gayle-Evans, 2022).

African American grandmothers play a variety of roles. They are known to nurture their grandchildren and will readily assist with child care, if needed. It is also not unusual for African American grandmothers to play the role of surrogate parent to their grandchildren. They are also expected to "co-parent," to provide guidance and discipline, even if they do not reside with their grandchildren. The African American grandmother is typically considered an extended member of her family and is very highly valued. She is usually recognized as the matriarch as well as the "pillar" of her family. As in many other cultures, she is seen as a source of wisdom and is expected to provide continuation of the culture by transmitting customs and values (Gayle-Evans, 2022).

But the role of grandmother is not always relegated to biological grandmothers, as evidenced in many African American as well as some other cultures. In these cultures, elderly women are considered "grandmothers" and are treated the same way as biological grandmothers. In cultures such as Yemen, Oman, and Afghanistan, for example, children are taught at a very early age to respect the elderly whether or not they are related to them. Children are guided and disciplined by the elderly, and the children are expected to be obedient to them and treat them as they would treat their own grandparents.

However, as important as it is for the elderly to nurture their grandchildren, transmit cultural values, and assist with child-rearing, there are numerous other reasons for making sure that the elderly play a role in children's lives. Long-established research has shown the importance of contact between children and the elderly. According to research, young children who do not have much contact with the elderly, have shown a tendency to have a very negative attitude toward them (Sheehan, 1978; Kuehne, 1992; Strom & Strom, 1995; Park 2005; Conyers, 1996; Dallman & Power, 1997). Therefore, helping children learn about and be able to interact with the elderly can be quite beneficial. Children are more likely to develop a positive attitude toward elderly people when they know about them through interaction. They can learn for example, that the elderly are not frightening and interaction will help to remove any other negative views that young children sometimes have about the elderly.

But it is not always possible for children in Western cultures to connect with older adults, especially their grandparents. Studies have shown that many children do not live in close proximity to their grandparents and, in many instances, may also not have access to older adults (Leon & Leon, 1992; Kuehne, 1992; Conyers, 1996;

Hasson, 1996; Dallman & Power, 1997; Strom & Strom 1995). There is, also, the unfortunate situation where parents may be in conflict with their own parents and deliberately deny contact between the children and their grandparents.

To alleviate the problem and help young children make connections with the elderly, teachers and administrators, in some schools and childcare programs, have programs to facilitate interaction between children and the elderly. In some childcare programs, they have the *Grandma Program*. This is where older women come to the facility to interact with the children. Their role is typically one of "consoler" and nurturer. They are there to help the children, especially when the children are having a bad day. One teacher, Hasson (1996), wrote of her experience of not having access to her grandparents. She therefore created an activity for *Grandparents' Day*, for children in her classroom who did not have access to their grandparents.

However, researchers have found that it is not only children who benefit from interaction with the elderly. Studies have shown that older adults also benefit from interaction with young children. Older adults with dementia have also been shown to benefit from interaction with young children. Some facilities for older adults offer childcare to ensure intergenerational interaction which they consider beneficial to both the children and the older adults (Heerema, 2022).

The United States, in an attempt to show recognition for the elderly and to celebrate them, established *National Grandparents Day*. This is celebrated the first Sunday after Labor Day. There is also *National Gorgeous Grandma Day,* which is celebrated on July 23rd of each year.

f

Preface

For many grandmothers, their role, whether defined or not, is not complicated. Typically, what most grandmothers want to do is to give to their grandchildren what they believe they did not give to their children. For example, spending time with them. Many women, while raising their children, are preoccupied with jobs outside the home and taking care of the needs of their families. First-time mothers have the task of learning how to take care of their child. This can be quite daunting. Grandmothers, on the other hand, come to the role with experience and confidence. Many will be there as a support and guide for parents, especially new parents, but others prefer to remain on the periphery. They make suggestions and give advice. Some will even give advice when not asked. Also, because it is not their child, they can afford to enjoy the relationship in what many may find to be "stress-free," if there are no concerns within the family. As one grandmother described the situation: "It's free rein. I take my grandchildren, we have fun, and then I give them back." However, they do worry about their grandchildren. They want to make sure they are in a safe, healthy, and loving environment, and many grandmothers will be the first to intervene if they detect that their grandchild is experiencing any challenges.

The warmth and caring that grandmothers feel for their grandchildren, can extend to any child. As an early childhood educator, I watched with interest the interaction between the older women and children in the *Grandma Program* in childcare centers where I worked. The women did not know the children and, initially, the children did not know the "Grandma," yet the children were willing to seek solace from these *Grandmas*, and the women were willing to console these children just as they would for their own grandchildren. It was fascinating and a joy to watch. This was one of the reasons for engaging in this project. What I saw was a story worth telling. The second reason for this project is my interest in multicultural education. Grandmothers are universal. The race or cultural background of the children and the *Grandmas* was of little importance. The need to nurture or the children's need to be nurtured was what was important. It was awe-inspiring. Grandmothers, it became clear, are similar in many ways. Grandmothers, regardless of culture, race, or language, nurture children, provide guidance as needed, babysit if necessary, and are an anchor in many families. I felt a strong need to pay tribute to them.

The idea of a tribute was easy enough. However, it was not immediately clear to me what to do or how to do it. I initially started by collecting names that are used to refer to grandmothers. I asked my colleagues, students I taught, and friends, to provide me with names for their grandmother, as well as other names that they knew. I became fascinated with the fact that there were so many different names for grandmother, even within one culture. As I worked on this, my interest in the topic piqued. Here we have a universal, grandmothers, who are similar in so many ways, yet they are so different, not only in how they are referred to by their grandchildren but also in some of the roles that they play. It was then that I decided that I would write poems that pay tribute to grandmothers, but I would write the poems from the perspective of children.

As I researched grandmothers and their roles, I realized that there are many poems written to and about grandmothers. Therefore, for this project, I decided to use the alphabet and incorporate it with different cultures. I chose a culture or country that began with each letter of the alphabet from A-Z. I then researched the culture looking especially at the language, food, clothing, cultural traits, challenges, politics, the role of the grandmother and childcare. Each poem was then written from the perspective of a child from that culture.

Like many people, I did not know my grandparents, so I empathize with those who grow up without their grandparents. However, I had access to elderly family members and family friends, so I felt comfortable with the topic of grandparents. I had collected the names for grandmothers and began to work on the project. However, as I delved into the research, I realized that being a grandmother was not necessarily what I had perceived it to be. I had taken for granted my knowledge of who really is a grandmother. That had changed.

Unlike the typical traditional grandmother whose role was mainly nurturing or babysitting, many grandmothers had to become more engaged in the lives of their grandchildren. The AIDS epidemic, and other social problems, began to surface. Changes in drug laws and drug use and abuse meant more incarceration for men and women. Other issues such as the increasing divorce rate and teenage pregnancy impacted plans for retirement for many women. Many grandmothers were being put in a position where they now had to provide greater assistance in taking care of their grandchildren or become "parents" for their grandchildren. Some who had retired had to come out of retirement and return to work while many others had to support their grandchildren on their small pensions (Smith, 1999; Park,

2005; Smith, Dannison & Vach-Hasse, 1998 Pantagraph, Ill, 1998). There was a sense of urgency. I felt the need to focus on the role of grandmothers; the joys that they are feeling, as well as the sacrifice that so many of these women are making for their children and grandchildren.

Conclusion

Although the poems are written as a tribute to grandmothers and can be used, generally, as a poetry book, there are also many other ways in which the material can be used. Because insight is given on a variety of cultures, the content strongly supports studies in diverse cultures and studies in multicultural education. The content also strongly supports the literature and social studies curriculum. There is reference to the impact of issues such as the AIDS epidemic (South Africa, Zimbabwe), the family with the grandmother as head of household or as a member of the extended family and intergenerational relationships. Also covered, from the point of view of social studies, is the topic of "enduring issues" such as poverty and women's issues/rights, such as voting.

Every attempt has been made to provide an accurate representation of each culture. Information received from persons I interviewed, such as friends from The Dominican Republic, Ghana, Panama, Turkey, Morocco and India, for example, was verified with other available sources. Also, information I received from strangers I interviewed was also checked for authenticity. In some instances, such as the name for grandmother, various names were provided. I therefore tried to use the one that seemed more popular and recognizable.

The process for this project has been an amazing and exciting journey. I can only hope that readers will enjoy it as much as I have enjoyed working on it. I also hope that the material will encourage the reader to delve deeper into the cultures mentioned and even the many cultures that I did not include.

* None of the characters in the poems are real. However, the information in each poem is meant to convey a true and important aspect of that culture.

* Please note that some of the studies included in this work have been referenced in other works by the author.

The Poems

These poems are written as a tribute to grandmothers everywhere. There are over forty poems. The poems are written in alphabetical order from A to W, Y and Z with each letter of the alphabet representing a culture or country (there is no country beginning with the letter "X"). However, in some cases, there are two or more poems for the culture or country, for example, Liberia and the United States.

Each poem is an attempt to capture the relationship between a grandmother and grandchild from each of the countries/cultures represented. The poems are written from the perspective of children of different ages. Some of the poems represent younger children while others represent much older children.

The poems are based on research and interviews related to cultures, which include the Dominican Republic, Ghana, Hungary, India, Morocco, Poland, Russia and Turkey, as well as personal knowledge derived from visits by some of the contributors to the following countries: Australia, Barbados, Canada, Cuba, England, France, Haiti, Italy, Jamaica, Mexico, Nigeria, Panama, Vietnam and Wales.

In each instance, the poet has tried to capture the culture, using the information acquired, and then write each poem from that cultural group's perspective.

Acknowledgment

There are several persons who were directly or indirectly involved with this project, to whom I am deeply grateful. Thanks to my sisters Ms. Casseia Sinclair and Ms. Venus McGregor-Lowe for your constant support and encouragement. I also have to say special thanks to you Venus for staying up that night in Panama to listen as I excitedly shared some of my favorite poems. To the students and colleagues at the University of South Florida St. Petersburg who willingly shared their culture or that of their relatives with me, I am truly grateful. Thanks to the many strangers I met on the street, who gladly stopped when asked and spent their time with me to tell me about their culture and their grandmothers. Many thanks also to my friends from Ghana, Hungary, Puerto Rico, and other cultures who so willingly shared information with me and did not mind when I needed more details.

Very special thanks to my sisters Dr. Lena Hall and Dr. Noga Gayle for, first of all, so gladly and willingly agreeing to make direct contributions when asked. Dr. Hall chose to write a poem for *England, Germany* and *Italy* and Dr. Gayle chose *France, Haiti, South Africa and Vietnam*. I would also like to thank them for their undying support throughout my work on this project. I am really, truly grateful. Thanks, also, for agreeing to read the work and providing me with such wonderful suggestions. I am more grateful than you will ever know. Many thanks are also due to my friend and colleague Dr. Juanita Fountain at the University of South Florida St. Petersburg, who, when asked, also willingly contributed two poems - *Brazil* and the first poem about *Liberia*. There are just not enough words to express my appreciation and gratitude to all of them for their support and their contributions.

Last, but certainly not least, thanks to the memory of my parents Charles and Leanora Gayle who never imposed restrictions on my need to be creative. Thanks for giving me wings and constantly reminding me that the sky is my only limit.

For Grandmothers Everywhere!

Grandmother, grandmother, where can you be?

Canada? Mexico? Somewhere in the Caribbean, maybe?

You like Ocho Rios, Jamaica. Is that where you are?

Dominican Republic, Cuba, or are you in Panama?

Are you in Australia, Haiti, South Africa, maybe?

Poland, Russia, or Zimbabwe?

Wherever you are, grandmother, I no longer want to guess

I just want you to know that you are greatly missed.

Be safe and come back soon from wherever you are.

I need you as you have always been my guiding star.

I miss you, dear grandma, and I'm trying to let you know,

Through these poems written about you,

That I love you so.

My Grandmother

My grandmother, she's so fine,

She plays with me all the time,

Kisses my boo-boo, when I am hurt,

I tell you,

She's the best grandmother on earth.

Afghanistan

My Afghanistani grandmother wears a *burka*,

Which, if you do not know,

It is a type of clothing

That covers her from head to toe.

"*Maadar Bozorg*," I said quite cheerily,

"Why don't you show your pretty face?"

"It's tradition," She said softly,

In a voice I did not know,

And not being able to see her face,

I couldn't tell if it were really so.

"I wear my *burka* proudly,"

She then added after a short while.

"Will I get to wear one?"

I asked her with a smile.

She paused and then I added,

"But if I get to wear one, I want my face to show."

"You are my American grandchild," she answered.

"And so, quite frankly, I don't know."

Australia

Australian grandmother,

Nice as can be,

Makes *vegemite* sandwiches

Just for me.

Some people don't like *vegemite*,

I know that for sure,

But grandmother and I like *vegemite*

More than you'll ever know!

Barbados

My Barbadian grandmother,

Always busy as can be.

"Come on, child, we must hurry," she would always say to me.

"Got to get you to school early,

Teacher says you can't be late another day."

Then, I would quickly put on my school uniform

While she straightened out my braids.

"Don't forget your lunch," she would say

As I headed for the door.

Then, I would grab my lunch box.

I tell you, those days were the best, for sure.

Brazil

My *Avó* was lots of fun

As she allowed me to play and

keep on the run..

We went for a walk almost everyday

Where she pointed out things that I remember today.

Happy was I with her close by my side

To tend to my hurts and comfort my cries.

My mother had to work every day,

But my grandmother was there to show me the way.

Those early years I remember so clearly.

I remember the music, the laughter, and the tears.

She was there in my early years.

When I was so busy learning about the world,

She encouraged my learning.

She provided me with the wings to navigate the sky,

But I am sure she did not realize how high I would fly.

I truly thank her for those early years

When I was fleet of foot,

And she was a quiet spirit and a masterful cook.

Happy were those days for me,

I look back with such fondness, joy and glee,

Though I know you cannot remember much now

Because the years have stolen many of those precious memories.

Canada

Canadian grandmother,

Oh, what a sight!

Helping me and my brother

Fly our kite.

We are at Centre Island, a park,

It's a good place to be

"Release the cord slowly," she reminds us with glee.

Now watch as the kite climbs up high.

"Oh look!" my brother shouts as he points toward the sky

"There are cotton clouds," he says, "way up high!

Floating, floating, under the blue sky!"

Cuba

Cuban *Abuela*,

Generous with her smile,

She approaches to see if I am alright.

"Qué pasa?" she asks, but I can only smile.

I cannot explain that I am thirsty and tired.

"Agua, por favor?" I manage to say

In an accent that surely gave me away.

"Tourista?" She asks. I nod to say "Yes."

What else she needs to know

I won't even guess.

She goes back inside and then reappears

With a clear glass of water,

I am almost in tears.

"Gracias, gracias." I manage to say,

As I quenched that thirst I thought would never go away.

Dominican Republic

Today is a very happy day

For me and my sister Maria.

Soon we will be going to the Dominican Republic to visit our
Abuela.

When we left for the United States, I was five and she was three.

Of course, she didn't get it, but it was a sad day for me.

I haven't seen my *Abuela* since,

And now I am almost nine, so my mother thinks that it is definitely
about time.

She thinks the need to connect with our Dominican family has gone
way overtime.

We leave in two weeks,

When school breaks for Christmas vacation.

Christmas time with Abuela,

What a celebration it's going to be

Eating *La bandera* and *sancocho*, two of my favorite meals.

Christmas, is usually a wondrous time

When friends and family gather.

My friend Teresa is also coming, I can't wait to see her.

Teresa is a few months younger than me,

But that doesn't really matter.

Mama says that we are more like sisters,

We have been friends since we were toddlers.

I know some Spanish but not a whole lot,

"Buenos dias" "buenos tardes" and things like that,

But I am not worried.

The best thing is going to be the time spent together,

Abuela, Maria, Teresa and me.

Egypt

The streets of Cairo,

As busy as can be,

But in my mind,

It's just my *Tita* and me.

She is taking me shopping with her

For the very first time.

She always said I wasn't old enough to go,

But today she said: "It's time!"

We cross on many cross walks,

There are lights red, yellow and green,

And walk past fruit and merchant stands,

It is a sight to be seen.

We stop at a merchant's stand

Where they're selling head scarves.

She looks at a few of them

And then she laughs.

"I am not paying that price for that!" she says,

But as she is about to leave,

The owner says: "Stop, lady, don't go, please."

"I can give you a better price," he continues with a smile.

As she turns to go back, she says,

"Oh, that's nice."

So, she walks back to the merchant's stand

And picks a scarf that is colorful and bright.

She then pays the merchant

Without fuss or fight.

She takes my hand, we're off once more.

My only wish

Is that our next stop

Will be a food stand, for sure.

England

My English Grandmother.

"Grandma, Grandma." I shouted real loud,

Worming my way through the airport crowd.

I had spotted my grandma waiting for me

To spend time with her in London City.

I was born in America and had never been there,

But grandma would visit me once every year.

On the way to her home, grandma showed me Big Ben,

The double Decker buses, and the English children.

The next day I went to see Queen Elizabeth's Palace,

And made friends with a little girl named Alice.

She was the same age as me, and oh so polite.

I wondered if she would ever kick, scream, or fight.

The changing of the guards was demonstrated so neatly.

I clapped and I cheered, Alice only smiled sweetly.

All summer I ate crumpets, drank tea like a lady,

Said "Yes, please" and "Thank you" and "Actually, maybe."

My grandma was tickled at my speech imitation

Of her accent, her phrases, and voice modulation.

The whole summer was great, grandma is a trooper.

I hope and pray I will never ever lose her.

France

Every summer no one needs to remind me

That it's time to visit my dearest Mamie.

She lives in the south of France in the beautiful town

Of Perpignon, close to the border with Spain.

Landscape painting has been her hobby since she could spell her name,

We are constantly walking around with palettes,

Paints, canvases, water, easels and brushes,

Looking for suitable spots to relax and paint in the bushes.

One day we went across the border by train

To Figueres, a small town in Spain.

We visited Salvador Dali's Museum in all its splendor,

After hours in the museum it was time to surrender.

Mamie took me to lunch, and oh what a treat,

From the café we watched interesting people walking up and down the street.

On returning to Mamie's home, we continued to enjoy the great climes,

I quickly realized the coming to the end of our good times,

But the wonderful memories are what I will hold dear

while looking forward to the same time next year.

Germany

Oma, my German grandmother.

On weekdays, *Oma* picks me up after school,

While I wait for my Mom, there is only one rule.

"Do your homework, and then you can watch TV

Good students have grades higher than a B."

Oma would give me milk, sausage, and bread.

"Please, *Oma*, instead of sausage, can I have

cheese instead?"

Oma obliges. She is a doting grandmother.

It is hard to believe *Oma* raised my own mother.

Mother loves me, I know, but ignores all my pining.

She calls my requests silly, *childish whining*.

If I ask to stay up and watch a late TV show,

"Oh no," says my mom, "You need sleep to grow."

If I tell her, "*Oma* lets me do what I want to do,"

She says, "That's *Oma*. Too bad! Goodnight and I love you."

Ghana

"*Adiki*, *Adikwo*, come here," she would say.

We knew what it meant, hair-threading day.

My *Nana Baa*, on my father's side,

Was from the large Andangme tribe,

And she was upset that he chose an Akan tribe,

So she tried often and as best as she could

To raise us Adangme in language, customs, and food.

But what seemed to matter to her the most

Is that we learn Ghana hair-threading

So that she could boast that although we

Were Andangmen only by half,

We knew the language and customs, so all

Was not totally lost.

So, on days such as this, week after week,

She would thread our hair, like clockwork,

For it was quite a treat.

She would start with my sister, for reasons I still don't know,

Then she would talk as she worked, it was quite a show.

"You need to wind it tightly

At the root," she would say,

"You cannot decide to do it any old way!"

Then she would move her fingers quickly

As she wound the thread around the clump of hair she had selected,

Long, curly, and dark brown.

"Now keep wrapping the thread around until you get to the end,

Then tie a knot in the thread.

See, it's not as hard as you think."

Then she would move to the next clump of hair

And repeat the same action. Had to be done to *Nana Baa's*
satisfaction.

I watched fascinated even though I had seen this many times before,

But my sister would stifle her yawns, I think she was bored.

However, as I look back at this, I now realize,

It was not the hair threading

That I would give the prize.

It was the time *Nana Baa* spent working hard to ensure

That our cultural identity

With the Andangme tribe would endure.

Haiti

Although many may dismiss our beloved Haiti as a lost cause,

Little do they know that our families are as closely woven as gauze.

Our dear *Gogo* is our rock,

And the stories she tells us no one would mock.

She tries to keep our family as stable as she is able.

She can speak French, English and Creole.

She even understands African American Soul.

Our *Gogo* is an artist as many Haitians are.

She paints, she carves, and is a singer in her own right.

We are pleased to salute our *Gogo*, every day and every night.

Hungary

Time in Palatinus,

Sometimes several hours at a time,

Sliding down the waterfall,

Nagymama watched me, she didn't mind.

Took me to school and picked me up,

Read me stories at night.

Made sure I felt safe when my parents were not around,

And she did this all with a smile.

On some days, I remember,

As if she read my mind

She would make *Hungarian gulyás* or *csirke paprikás*

These are still favourite foods of mine.

India

My *Nanni*, slender, kind,

She wears a sari all the time,

Beautiful saris with threads of gold,

Various colors, some pastel some bold.

"Nanni," I say, "I want to look like you!"

"You will, one day!" she says,

"I promise you!"

Ireland

"Loop one, loop two,

Ah, but don't make it so tight.

You need to make room for the needle and next loop.

Don't you remember, we have to do this right?"

"Oh, *Maimeó*, I just can't do this," I softly said.

I was almost in tears as I kept shaking my head.

"Oh, don't say that my Shauna," she said with a smile.

"Keep trying, you can do it."

She didn't seem to understand my plight.

But just then she said,

"Let me show you once again.

Crocheting is easy, my Shauna,

You just need to be more patient."

She took the needle and thread from me gently

And showed me the stitch once more.

I moved closer to her,

This time I wanted to get it for sure.

Now as I look back at those early days,

When learning to crochet almost left me in a daze,

I have to say thanks to

That wonderful *Maimeó* of mine,

For now, I love to crochet,

It's my most favorite pastime.

Italy

Nona, my Italian Grandmother.

I love to spend time at my Nona's home.

We travel there from our house in Rome.

Nona's home is in Venice. It's so pleasing to the eye,

I would sit by the window and watch gondolas go by.

Nona feeds me pasta and milk made from soy

To help me, she says, to grow up to be a big boy.

Nona likes to take me for walks on the street

So she can show me off to the friends she might meet.

She tells them I am handsome, and smart, and real good,

That when I am around her, she is in a good mood.

She tells me it's a good habit to walk, and not drive.

That these healthy habits will keep us alive.

I pretend not to notice there are no cars on the street,

So we laugh, walk, and talk until we both are quite beat.

Back at *Nona's*, I wait for my mom to come get me

While I drink homemade fruit juice and eat ravioli.

Jamaica

Jamaican grandmother,

Elegant, proud,

Never one to speak out loud,

Always a lady, no matter what,

Church going, kind, gentle, and that's a fact.

No Hip-Hop music in her house,

Some reggae is allowed if it's not too loud.

Drives me to school,

Will pick me up too,

Constantly tells me, "I am so proud of you!"

Kenya

Kenyan grandmother,

Sweet as can be.

When mama goes to work,

She takes care of my brother *Akello* and me.

She walks us to school everyday,

And even waits till we are settled,

And sometimes for lunch,

She makes our favorite,

Madake or (*posho) porridge.*

She is always gentle, and she is always kind,

And she always greets everyone with a smile.

On special occasions, when friends and family gather,

Akello, our cousins, and I like to stay close to grandmother,

Who will secretly give us extra helpings of *nyama choma.*

Akello and I and our cousins agree,

There is no one in the world like our *Bibi.*

Liberia (1)

Grandmother, as I look out upon our ravaged and war-torn land,

I remember how you quieted my fears on every hand.

The stories you told were about happier times,

When my mother was young and you were in your prime.

You talked about your home-life and the people in your village,

The beauty of the land and the beauty of the countryside,

Where you gathered food before it was pillaged.

Your voice was always strong, loving, kind, and sweet,

As I listened to you I could visualize every street.

My mother and I are fortunate to a have someone like you,

One who has shown tremendous courage

In the face of daily suffering and widespread hunger and pain.

You managed to bring us laughter, joy, and hope,

in spite of the enormous strain.

I will forever remember you fondly,

Even though I may be far away,

I carry the stories you so skillfully told

To pass on to my children each day.

I saw the past events through the lens you provided,

And understand the present…

Liberia (2)

My grandmother wears a *lappa*,

And she speaks to me in *kru*.

My grandmother is Liberian, and I don't know what to do.

I am American born and raised, and visiting Liberia, as my
grandmother says,

"To learn the ways of my people and learn to say with pride, I am
Liberian American, until the day I die."

She is teaching me to "*snapshake*" so I won't look like a fool

When I go with her to visit her friends, and she does have quite a
few.

The food here is great, but it's not all new to me.

I have eaten this type of food, since I was at my mother's knee—

Dumboy, cassava leaves, grains, *fufu* and rice.

My grandmother says that nowhere is there food that is this nice.

I am having a good time, and my grandmother is quite pleased

That I enjoy playing the *gowd* and dancing to the Liberian beat.

I only have one problem though, that grandmother chooses to
ignore,

I wish she'd speak to me in English,

So I would be able to understand and say more.

Mexico

"¿Cómo está usted? " she says

As we stand face to face.

But I can only stare at her as if I am staring into space.

"Don't be sad," she whispers.

"My beautiful *Teresita*,

I will come back to see you in the not too distant future."

"*Abuela*," I say. "You just don't know – the time I've spent with you

Has taught me so much about Mexico."

You see, my father is from Mexico, my mother Mexican-American,

And I am trying to learn as much about Mexico as I possibly can.

My *Abuela* smiles and then she strokes my face.

We're at the airport, it's time for her to go to the gate.

After much hugging and kissing, she slowly walks away.

She is as sad as I am. It's what she would call a "good-bad" day.

"Muchas gracias, *Abuela*," I whisper,

"And there's no need for you to fear

Because I will always remember the things you told me

And how you showed how much you cared.

And, who knows, Dear *Abuela*,

Maybe I'll see you again next year!"

Morocco

I remember it well.

It was a wonderful time,

Visiting my *Ljeda* in Morocco

For the first time,

Finally fulfilling a long-awaited dream of mine.

It was a dream that I had ever since the time

That I learned that

Morocco was part of my ancestral line.

I went to food markets, as well as tourist sites,

Casablanca, Rabat, and other places that filled me with delight.

But the times spent at home with *Ljeda*

Were some of the best,

Stories of the past, family life, customs

And the way people dress.

She made the best harira soup that I have ever known,

And with mutton, a type of meat I had not yet known, I couldn't
wait to tell all this

As soon as I got back home.

I had couscous which is made from seminola grain.

My *Ljida* teased and said, "It's good for the brain."

But what I enjoyed most though,

And this may seem strange,

Was playing *"Fox and Rabbit"*

A common Moroccan game.

Nicaragua

Bags of clay on the side and

Wet clay on the table,

Abuela sitting on the stool

With the kick wheel going as fast as she is able.

Oh, I can see it forming now

As I watch *Abuela's* soppy hands work.

I think, at first, it's a bowl, no, it's a vase,

Or maybe it is just a very large cup.

I usually cannot tell what it is

Until the spinning wheel stops.

Abuela's hands are working so fast

That I can hardly keep up.

I try to keep guessing, I will not give up

Until *Abuela* lifts her foot and the spinning wheel finally stops.

The kiln is, of course, fired up.

It's hot and it's ready to accept

Whatever unique piece of pottery

Abuela has thrown next.

I am allowed to make things
That I can safely mold by hand.
I can even dip them in the glaze
Under *Abuela's* watchful guidance.

No spinning wheels or kiln for me,
I can only watch and wait to see,
And maybe even try to imagine
What the item will turn out to be.

Nigeria

My Mama died of AIDS when I was eight,
And that left me and my *Jayplo* in quite a state.
Now it's just my *Jayplo* and me,
We are all that's left of our family.

My *Jayplo* does her best, but it is very hard,
Raising a child at her age, is quite a task.
Making *garri* or cooking chicken stew for us to eat,
Shopping or making clothes for herself and for me.

We both realize these are difficult tasks,
Far more than anyone would ask,
But my *Jayplo*, she never complains.
Fussing about it, she says, is all in vain.

So my *Jayplo* she works hard
To make sure life for me is fine.
She keeps telling me over and over, time after time,
That maybe things will get better
By the time I am nine.

Oman

What great excitement it was for me
To visit the country of my ancestry.
My mother's mother lives in Oman,
To visit her was the plan.
But things do not always go the way we like.
I visited with my *Jadda* and here was my plight.
My *Jadda* speaks mostly Arabic, but I didn't have a clue,
So I spoke English as many of the Omani people do.

I feasted on fruit, bread, and rice,
I even ate *helwa* made with honey and spice,
I joined my cousin's small pottery class,
And we made strange looking clay pots,
Which made my *Jadda* laugh.
But she said, "At least you're busy and not just goofing off."

This sounded really funny, as I am sure you may have guessed.
But I really enjoyed my time in Oman.
My *Jadda* is the best.

Pakistan

My *Jaddah* wears a *burka*,

She's covered almost from head to toe.

"Why do you wear that, *Jaddah*?" I ask.

"Is there something you don't want the world to know?"

"It's my religion and a custom,"

She explains to me.

"There's nothing that I do not want all the world to see.

You're young, you do not get it,

But one day you'll understand.

The *burka* and the *hijab*

Are just some of the traditions of Pakistan."

Panama

Panamanian *Abuela*,

Hearty, proud, yet kind,

She is definitely one of a kind.

Came to the United States

For her grandson's college graduation,

She said, "He is my first grandchild to

Get this far with education."

He threw her a kiss, and he also waved

As he walked proudly across the stage,

Diploma held high in his hand,

Although he couldn't even see her in the stands.

His *Abuela* is gone now, but he'll never forget

How proud she was of him and his academic success.

Poland

My dearest *Babcia*,

What can I say?

Read me stories almost every day.

A Holocaust survivor, yet she never complained,

Just shared some stories of the pain.

Holidays were special, especially Name Days and weddings,

But also, ordinary days when we ate

Gotabki, pieorgi, and my favorite, cabbage.

But none of the days can ever compare

To Christmas Eve Supper, that very special time of the year.

It is usually a family gathering, a part of tradition,

Sharing *oplatek*, fish, noodles, and another of my favorite, wheat
pudding.

The times spent with *Babcia*,

So filled with fun and delight,

They are memories that I will treasure

For the rest of my life.

Puerto Rico

My *Abuela*, Maria was her name,

Served us *arroz con pollo y pasteles*

At her house, after almost every baseball game.

It didn't matter if we won or lost—

At *Abuela's* house we weren't allowed to make a fuss,

Or behave in unsportsmanlike ways,

Or she would remind us that we are a team,

And it is only a game.

Unfortunately, *Abuela's* gone now,

But what we have gained

Is an angel cheering our team

At every game.

Qatar

It's voting day in Qatar,

And it wouldn't be that special

Except that now women are allowed to vote

After many years of repression.

My *Jadda* is excited.

"Come on," she says excitedly, "We don't want to be late."

I didn't really get it because I am from the United States.

I am visiting Qatar for a while,

So, of course, I found this all interesting,

Since women voting in the United States

Is so often taken for granted.

In the United States, voting is the norm,

Both men and women have been voting

Since before my *Jadda* was born.

My *Jadda* and I get to the polling station,

There is excitement everywhere,

Women in their finest clothing,

It's like the best time of the year.

My *Jadda* is the next in line,

So, she goes into the booth.

She says it is like losing your very first tooth.

She marks her ballot, then closes her eyes,

She wants to remember this very special time.

"I've done it! I've done it!" she whispers and then smiles.

"I have exercised my right.

A right for which so many others

Have had to pay such an enormous price."

Russia

Being with my *Babushka*

Was for me always a treat.

She read me stories after a day at work

As she rested her tired feet.

Later, after a dinner of boiled potatoes, *Kolbasa*, or sausage and
bread,

We would play a game of *durak*

Before she sent me off to bed.

Sometimes we ate Russian honey cake

Just before we played our game,

And, usually, for me, that was the best time of the day.

On weekends, my *Babushka* and I

Would drive for an hour to the *dacha*.

This is another special time that we liked to spend together.

We worked in her small garden, something

We both liked to do

While she talked to me about life,

I could only talk about my week at school.

But she listened quite intently, something I came to expect,
My wonderful *Babushka* always treats me with respect.

I love her so much yet I can hardly describe
How happy I am that my *Babushka* was and still is
An important part of my life.

South Africa

As one of many orphans in South Africa,

I gladly sing the praises of my grandmother,

After happily raising her sons and daughters,

She is now a living witness to the AIDS disaster.

She buries her own children who

Were our fathers and mothers,

She cares for us without bother.

She does this with honor and grace,

We see this expressed by the pleasure on her face.

We know raising us is not an easy task,

So we try to create a peaceful environment in which she can bask.

Tanzania

"Stand still, child, and don't you wriggle.

I have to get this right,

For if I don't, this uniform will end up too big or too tight.

It's only two weeks, you know,

Before your school begins,

And your *Bibi* cannot go as fast as she used to.

Please hand me two of those pins."

I hardly hear my *Bibi* because I am as excited as can be.

I am finally going to learn to read and write and do arithmetic.

I promise myself that as soon as I learn to do all these important things,

I will teach my brother Abasi and my sisters *Afya* and *Adin*.

"Now turn around and let me do the back," *Bibi* says as she pats my leg.

I turn and I know my *Bibi* didn't see on my face, the world's biggest grin.

In two weeks, I'll have my new uniform, and I will also be in school.

My *Bibi* has no idea she's making me the happiest girl in the world.

Turkey

My *Nani* was coming to the United States

To live with my family.

Mama said she was coming

So she could help to take care of my sister Adile and me.

I had lived with my *Nani* until I was the age of five,

And though it may be hard to believe,

Now, I am almost nine.

My *Nani* was excited,

But as Mama explained,

It was her first time traveling alone

On an airplane.

As you can imagine, I could hardly wait

For my *Nani's* arrival in the United States.

I remember also thinking

That I can't wait to eat

Borek, *Kebob*, *and Dolma*,

Traditional Turkish foods

That were my favorite treat.

As I waited, I made her drawings,

And I wrote her very short notes,

So that as mother suggested, I would not "explode".

It seemed like years

As I anxiously waited for my *Nani* to arrive

So that I could once again experience

The good times I had with her

From birth till the age of five.

Ukraine

Sunday market in *Kiev,*

What a treat!

Lots of people

Out shopping in the street.

Not like Saturday market

Where I am from,

It's a different kind of order

But definitely more fun.

Me and my *Baba,*

We walk round and round,

Looking for bargains

And a lot could be found.

Baba bought mushrooms, various vegetables,

And my favorite, poppy seeds,

Some items for *borsch,*

And some other foods that we would need.

Then it was off to the butcher's
And other food stands down the street
To buy the meat, fowl, and fish
That we would need for the week.

United States

My *Nana* was eventually approved

To come to live with us,

But before all this could happen,

There was just a little fuss.

At first some of the officials

Became quite frantic and caused a little uproar because, as they indicated,

They really were not sure

If any other grandmother

Had lived in this important house before.

So, they had to think about it,

And they all had to agree,

Whether *Nana* could come and live with us

In this important house in Washington, D. C.

But my parents were determined,

Having *Nana* there was a must.

They were not willing to accept any ifs, ands, or buts.

Then one day the officials called and said that they had all agreed,

Yes, it was a unanimous decision

That *Nana* could live with us in D. C.

So that she could help to take care of my sister and me.

Now, just in case you are wondering,

There are things that you should know.

She is just the same grandmother that she was before,

A grandmother who worries and fusses over us and who we just adore.

She likes to help our mother make sure we are alright and,

Like our mother, likes to read to us at night.

We really love you, *Nana*, and we are so glad that you are here.

Thank you for your warm smiles, your love, and constant care.

We really feel very special and grateful

That you agreed

To leave your home and good friends in Chicago

And come to live with us in Washington, D. C.

United States

It has been decided,

They now all agree,

That our *Nana* can move in with

My mother, father, sister, and me.

It took some exploring,

Was it ever done before?

Yes, they did find precedence

We needn't worry any more.

We all moved in, as expected,

Life is as normal as can be

In this wonderful, large house

In Washington, D. C.

There are a few things, however,

To which I have to get accustomed

We are constantly followed by men

In dark suits, dark glasses, and earplugs.

Men who have permission

To follow my sister and me to school,

To birthday parties and special functions,

All my friends think that's "cool".

My *Nana* assures me

That this is all fine.

One day I will look back

And smile at these times.

"And, anyway," she reminds me,

"It is only four more years to make eight.

You will be out of this situation

By the time you are old enough to go on dates."

United States - African American

My Grandmother, my *Meemaw*,

As busy as can be,

She is the pillar of our family.

Church on Sunday, then dinner at her home,

This is a tradition, and it is widely known.

We gather at the table and we try to eat really fast.

We can hardly wait to hear the stories

About days that have long passed–

Stories about segregation, integration, and "free at last."

"Life has changed," she would always say,

"Some for better, some for worse,

But I feel blessed to have you all here with me, in this house."

She would then take a deep breath, it almost is a sigh,

This would mean the stories are

About to begin–

I am now on a "Spiritual High!"

United States

My *Nana*, she takes care of my brother and me,

But it's not always fun and games.

She makes us take naps, even when it doesn't rain.

All in all though, she's as kind as can be,

For she kisses my "boo-boo" when I scrape my knee.

United States - Hawaiian

Mele Kalikimaha, it is that time of the year,

Christmas in Hawaii,

I can't wait to get there

To spend time with my *Tutu*

During Christmas and the New Year.

"*Meke Aloha*," I am greeted when I arrive

And given the most beautiful *lei*,

Which I am determined to wear with pride.

"*Aloha, aloha*," I keep saying,

I can hardly believe it's real,

That I am finally in Hawaii,

Right now, it's like a dream.

"Mo'opuna wahine," she will greet me at the gate.

Oh, to see my *Tutu* again, I can hardly wait.

Then suddenly, I see her and

My heart begins to beat real fast,

I am in Hawaii with my *Tutu*, at last!

Now learning to speak Hawaiian

Will be my greatest task.

Vietnam

Growing up in Vietnam is quite a challenge.

My *Bà* has experienced wars, destruction,

separation and unification.

She takes these changes in stride as she goes

about her chores.

I really enjoy accompanying her to the big

downtown stores.

We enter the market where vendors hawk their wares:

Lacquered furniture, pots, pans, carpets,

durian, mangosteen, and pears.

Our favourite spots are the stalls with silk dresses

Where we spend a lot of time talking with

the seamstresses.

Wales

Big day in cricket
For *Mam-gu* and me.
You see, *Mam-gu* is a bowler
On the Women's Cricket Team.

They practiced for months,
And now it is time
For this group of eleven
To go out and shine.

I've been working real hard
With homework and chores,
My reward for work well done
Will be spectator at this sport.

I will sit in the stands,
As I usually do,
And cheer *Mam-gu* on
And her ten friends too.

Yemen

My *Jadda* Hanan is special to me,

She has always been an important part of our family.

She taught me to make porridge and perfect sweet tea,

I watched her make *bint-as-sahn*, my favorite treat.

She taught me to sing and she taught me to dance

The *laheji* which often leaves me in some kind of trance.

When she is not busy and if I have been good,

She will join my cousins and me when we play *Quma Makshouf*.

Many times, she will console me

When my playmates call me names

Just because I couldn't remember the rules of the game.

My *Jadda* is as gentle as she is kind

But is firm about rules not being broken at any time.

She teaches school, and that's good for me.

She makes sure my work is always of the highest quality.

I have given it a lot of thought,

And I really don't know what my life would be

If it hadn't been for *Jadda* always looking out for me.

Zimbabwe

Toss one marble upward,

Using just one hand.

Then, with the other,

Grab as many marbles as you can. *Kudodo.*

"*Bibi*, this is hard to do," I say between my clenched teeth.

First I pick up one marble, then two and then only three.

"Just be patient!" *Bibi* says kindly, "Playing *Kudodo* is not hard.

We used to play it, as children, all the time in the backyard."

"Now try again, but on this try, toss the marble way up high."

I listen to her words and could not help but sigh.

I didn't believe that it would work, but I thought I should at least try,

Then I tossed the marble, as *Bibi* said, and I couldn't believe my eyes.

I was able to grab a handful of marbles. Once again, *Bibi* was right.

"Thank you, *Bibi*, thank you!" I say with a broad grin

Because I know now that,

When I next play with my friends,

I can definitely win.

APPENDIX A
Glossary

Arroz con gandules	Rice with pigeon peas
Bint-as-sahn	A puffy type pastry which is covered with honey
Bliny	Large, flat pastry (like pancakes)
Borek	Turkish pastry (thin layers of dough with either spinach or ground meat in each layer)
Borsch	A variety of soups
Couscous	A dish made with granulated seminola grains (usually eaten with meat and vegetables
Csirke paprikás	Chicken simmered in paprika
Dacha	Summer house
Dolma	Vegetables or leaves stuffed with or wrapped around rice or bulgar pilaf
Dumboy	Cassava roots which are boiled then beaten with a pestle
Durak	Card game
Durian	Big green thorny fruit. It is deliciously flavored but has a strong smell.
Fufu	Ground, fermented cassava that is boiled and served as soup
Garri	Powdered cassava
Gotabi	Dish of ground pork or beef and rice
Gowd	Dried gourd shell fitted between beads and used as a musical instrument
Helwa	Confectionary made with honey and spices
Hirira Soup	A National dish made with beef, mutton, water, and walnuts
Hungarian gulyás	Stuffed cabbage
Kebab	Meat roasted in pieces or slices on a skewer
Kolbasa	Hard cabbage
Kudodo	A game similar to Jacks which is played in several countries in Africa

La bandera	National dish of white rice and red beans and stewed meat usually served with fried plantain and vegetable
Laheji	A type of dance which originated in Lahj
Lappa	Colorful skirt made from hand–woven material
Madake	Banana porridge
Mangosteen	Reddish brown/purple fruit that is sweet and juicy
Nyama choma	Roasted meat
Oplatek	A thin white wafer
Pasteles	Plantain
Pieorgi	Pastry filled with potato, cheese, and meat or vegetable (like ravioli)
Posho	Porridge of ground corn
Quma Makshouf	Game of hide and seek
Sancocho	Stew with meat, plantain, and vegetable
Vegemite	Sandwich spread made from salty yeast

APPENDIX B
Word for Grandmother

Afghanistan	*Maadar-Bozorg (*Farsi & Persian) *Anaar* (Pashto)
Australia	*Grandmother, Grandmamma*, (various)
Barbados	*Grandma*
Brazil	*Avò*
Canada	*Grandma* (various)
Cuba	*Abuela*
Dominican Republic	*Abuela*
Egypt	*Tita*
England	*Grandma* (various)
France	*Grand-maman*
Germany	*Oma*
Ghana	*Nana Baa*
Haiti	*Gogo*
Hungary	*Nagymama*
India	*Nanni*
Ireland	*Maimeó*
Italy	*Nona* (a dialectical variation of "Nonna")
Jamaica	*Grandma*
Kenya	*Bibi*
Liberia	*Jayplo*
Mexico	*Abuela*
Morocco	*Ljeda*
Nicaragua	*Abuela*
Nigeria	*Jayplo*
Oman	*Jadda*
Pakistan	*Jaddah*
Panama	*Abuela*
Poland	*Babcia*
Puerto Rico	*Abuela*
Qatar	*Jadda*
Russia	*Babushka*

South Africa	*Gogo*
Tanzania	*Bibi*
Turkey	*Nani*
Ukraine	*Baba*
United States	*Grandma, Nana* (various)
United States	*Meemaw, Grandma,* (various)
United States (Hawaii)	*Tutu*
Vietnam	*Ba*
Wales	*Nain, mam-gu,* (various)
Yemen	*Jadda*
Zimbabwe	*Bibi*

APPENDIX C
Capital of Each Country

Afghanistan	*Kabul*
Australia	*Canberra*
Barbados	*Bridgetown*
Brazil	*Brasilia*
Canada	*Ottawa*
Cuba	*Havana*
Dominican Republic	*Santo Domingo*
Egypt	*Cairo*
England	*London*
France	*Paris*
Germany	*Berlin*
Ghana	*Accra*
Haiti	*Port-au-Prince*
Hungary	*Budapest*
India	*New Delhi*
Ireland	*Dublin*
Italy	*Rome*
Jamaica	*Kingston*
Kenya	*Nairobi*
Liberia	*Monrovia*
Mexico	*Mexico City*
Morocco	*Rabat*
Nicaragua	*Managua*
Nigeria	*Abuja*
Oman	*Muscat*
Pakistan	*Islamabad*
Panama	*Panama City*
Puerto Rico	*San Juan*
Poland	*Warsaw*
Qatar	*Doha*
Russia	*Moscow*
South Africa	*Pretoria*
Tanzania	*Dar es Salaam*

APPENDIX D
Children's Books About Grandmothers

Ada, A. (2002). *I Love Saturdays y Domingos*. New York: Aladdin Books.

Archambault, J. (1997). *Grandmother's Garden*. New York: Silver Press.

Bridges, S. (2002). *Ruby's Wish*. San Francisco: Chronicle Books.

Bunting, E. (1989). *The Wednesday Surprise*. New York: Clarion Books.

Bryan, A. (1977). *The Dancing Granny*. New York: Aladdin.

Carpenter, F. (2000). *Tales of a Korean Grandmother: 32 Traditional Tales from Korea*. New York: Tuttle Publishing.

Carpenter, F. (2001). *Tales of a Chinese Grandmother: 30 Traditional Tales from China*. New York: Tuttle Publishing.

Castaneda, O. S. (1993). *Abuela's Weave*. New York: Lee & Low.

Cech, J. (1991). *My Grandmother's Journey*. New York: Aladdin Paperbacks.

Christensen, B. (2003). *In My Grandmother's House*. New York: Harper Collins Children's Books.

Coleman, E. (1996). *White Socks Only*. Morton Grove, Ill: Albert Whitman and Co.

Crews, D. (1991). *Big Mama's*. New York: Greenwillow Books.

Cruise, R. (2006). *Little Mama Forgets*. New York, New York: Melanie Kroupa Books.

Daly, N. (1986). *Not So Fast Songololo*. New York: Puffin Books.

de Paola, T. (2002). *Adelita: A Mexican Cinderella Story*. New York: Puffin Books.

de Paola, T. (1973). *Nana Upstairs and Nana Downstairs*. New York: Puffin Books.

de Paola, T. (1996). *Strega Nona: Her Story*. New York: Puffin books.

Diouf, S. A. (2001). *Bintou's Braids*. San Francisco: Chronicle Books.

Dorros, A. (1991). *Abuela*. New York: Trumpet Books.

Duvall, D. L. (2003). *How Rabbit Lost His Tail: A Traditional Cherokee Legend (Grandmother Stories)*. Albuquerque, New Mexico: University of New Mexico.

Erdrich, L. (1996). *Grandmother's Pigeon*. New York: Hyperion Paperbacks for Children.

Fellows, R. (1998). *A Lei for Tutu*. Morton Grove, Illinois: Albert Whitman & Company.

Ferrin, W. W. (2002). *Grandmother's Alligator/Burukenge Wa Nyanya: A Tail in Two Sittings/Mkia Wa Vikao Viwili*. New York: Wakefield Connection.

Flournoy, V. (1985). *The Patchwork Quilt*. New York: Dial Books for Young Readers.

Fox, M. (1983). *Possum Magic*. New York: Voyager Books.

Garland, S. (1997). *The Lotus Seed*. New York: Voyager Books.

George, J. C. (1993). *Dear Rebecca, Winter is Here*. New York: Harper Collins.

Geras, A. (2003). *My grandmother's Stories: A Collection of Jewish Folktales*. New York: Alfred A. Knopf.

Greenfield, E. (1980). *Grandma's Joy*. New York: Penguin Putnam Books.

Grifalconi, A. (1986). *The Village of Round and Square Houses*. Boston: Little, Brown & Co.

Grimes, N. (2001). *Stepping with Grandma Mac*. New York: Orchard Books.

Hallinan, P. K. (2006). *Christmas at Grandma's House*. New York: Ideals Children's Books.

Hanel, W. & Unzer, C. (2002). *Weekend With Grandmother*. New York: Dial Books.

Hawxhurst, J. C. (1996). *Bubbe and Gram: My Two Grandmothers*. New York: Dovetail Publishing.

Hoffman, M. (1991). *Amazing Grace*. New York: Dial Books for Young Readers.

Hoffman, M. (1995). *Boundless Grace*. New York: Puffin Books.

Hughes, M. (1993). *A Handful of Seeds*. New York: Orchard Books.

Igus, T. (1996). *Two Mrs. Gibsons*. California: Children's Book Press.

Kessler, C. (2000) *My Great-Great grandmother's Gourd*. New York: Orchard Books.

Khalsa, D. K. (1986). *Tales of a Gambling Grandma*. New York: Dragonfly Books.

Krishnaswami, U. (2003). *Monsoon*. New York: Farrar Straus Giroux.

Lainez, R. C. (2005). *Playing Loteria: El Juego de la Loteria*. Flagstaff, AZ: Luna Rising.

Larrabee, L. (1996). *Grandmother Five Baskets*. New York: Roberts Rinehart Publisher.

Leitich-Smith, C. (2000). *Jingle Dancer*. New York: Morrow Junior Books.

Lyon, G. E. (1990). *Basket*. New York: Orchard.

Maclachlan, P. (2011). *Your Moon, My Moon: A Grandmother's Words to a Faraway Child*. Simon & Schuster Children's Publishing.

Martin, J. B. (2000). *Grandmother Bryant's Pocket*: New York: Houghton Mifflin Harcourt.

McCain, B. R. (1998). *Grandmother's Dreamcatcher*. Illinois: Albert Whitman and Co.

McElroy, L. T.; O'Connor, G.; Benjamin, J. (2000). *Meet My Grandmother: She's a Supreme Court Justice*. New York: IPicturebooks.

McKissack, P. C. (1988). *Mirandy and Brother Wind*. New York: Alfred A. Knopf.

McKissack, P. C. (2008). *Stitchin' and Pullin' a Gee's Bend Quilt*. New York: Random House.

McKissack, P. C. (2001). *Goin Someplace Special*. New York: Atheneum Books for Young Readers.

Mikolaycak, C. (1984). *Babushka*. New York: Holiday House.

Norac, I. (2009). *My Grandma is a Star*. New York: Macmillan Children's Books.

Older, E. (2000). *My Two Grandmothers*. New York: Harcourt Children's Books.

Onyefulu, I. (2010). *Grandma Comes to Stay*. Francis Lincoln Children's Books.

Oughton, J. (1996). *How the Stars Fall in the Sky: A Navajo Legend*. New York: Houghton Mifflin Harcourt.

Pak, S. (1999). *Dear Juno*. New York: Puffin Books.

Polacco, P. (1986*). Babushka's Doll*. New York: Simon & Schuster.

Polacco, P. (1992). *Chicken Sunday*. New York: Scholastic, Inc.

Polacco, P. (1992). *Mrs. Katz and Tush*. New York: Dell.

Polacco, P. (1988). *Rechenka's Eggs*. New York: The Putnam & Grosset Group.

Polacco, P. (1998). *The Keeping Quilt*. New York: Simon & Schuster Books for Young Readers.

Polacco, P. (1997). *Thunder Cake*. New York: Puffin Books.

Rattigan, J. (1993). *Dumpling Soup*. Boston: Little Brown and Company.

Root, P. (2002). *Big Momma Makes the World*. Massachusetts: Candlewick Press.

Ryan, P. (2000). *Esperanza Rising*. New York: Scholastic.

Ryan, P. M. (2001). *Mice and Beans*. New York, New York: Scholastic Press.

Rylant, C. (1982). *When I was Young in the Mountains*. New York: E. P. Dutton.

Sheth, K. (2007). *My Dadima Wears a Sari*. Atlanta: Peachtree Publishers.

Sisulu, E. B. (1996). *The Day Gogo Went to Vote*. N. Y: Little Brown and Co.

Skorpen, L. M. (1975). *Mandy's Grandmother*. New York: The Dial Press.

Taylor, M. (1976). *Roll of Thunder, Hear My Cry*. New York: Scholastic.

Tran, Am-Phong (2003). *Going Home, Coming Home*. New York: Children's Book Press.

Taulbert, C. (2001). *Little Cliff's First Day of School*. New York: Puffin Books.

Westheimer, R. (2001). *Dr. Ruth: Grandma on Wheels*. New York: Random house Children's Books.

Williams, V. A (1982). *Chair for My Mother*. New York: Scholastic, Inc.

Wyse, L. (1990). *Funny, You Don't Look Like a Grandmother*. New York: Harper Collins Publishers.

Wyse, L.; Goldman, M. R. (1998). *How to Take Your Grandmother to the Museum*. New York: Workman Publishing Co.

Young, E. (1989). *Lon-Po-Po: A Red-Riding Hood Story From China*. N. Y: Scholastic, Inc.

Zolotow, C. (1972). *William's Doll*. New York: Harper Collins.

Chapter Books (Older Children)

Crech, S. (1994). *Walk Two Moons*. New York: Harper Trophy.

Peck, R. (1997). *A Long Way from Chicago*. Scholastic, Inc.

Peck, R. (2000). *A Year Down Under*. New York: Scholastic, Inc.

References

Aday, R. H.; Sims, C. R. McDuffie, W., & Evans, E. (1996). Changing Children's Attitudes Toward the Elderly: The Longitudinal Effects of An Intergenerational Partners Program. *Journal of Research in Childhood Education*, 10, pgs. 143-51.

Apple, D. (1956). The Social Structure of Grandparenthood. *American Anthropologist*, 58(2), 656-63.

Baggett, S. (1981). Attitudinal Consequences of Older Adult Volunteers in the Public School6 Setting. *Educational Gerontology: An International Quarterly*, 7, 21-31.

Bales, S. Eklund, S. J., & Siffin, C. F. (2000).Children's Perceptions of Elders Before and After A School-Based Intergenerational Program. *Educational Gerontology*, 26(7), 677-89.

Conyers, J. (1996). Building Bridges Between Generations. *Educational Leadership*, 10(3), 14-16

Dallman, M. E. & Power, S. A. ((1997). Forever Friends: An Intergenerational Program. *Young Children*, 52(2), 64-8.

Entz, S. (1996). Somebody's Grandma. *First Teacher*, 17(2), 14-15.

Gayle-Evans, G. (2022). *The Role of Grandmothers as Presented in Multicultural Children's Literature: The Paradoxical Reality of Role Transformation in Diverse Cultures*. True Beginnings Publishing.

Gearon, , J. (2009). Grandparents Ride Seesaw Over Visitation Rights. *AARP Global Network*

Golden, M. (2009). Angel Baby. *Washingtonian*, 44(9), 21-4.

Hasson, J. B. (1996). Grandparent's Day: What to do for Children Who Don't Have a Grandparent. *Young Children*, 51(3), 28-31.

Heerema, E. (2022). Therapeutic Benefits of Children for People Living With Dementia. *Dotdash Media, Inc.*

Hoe, S. & Davidson, D. (2002). The Effects of Priming on Children's Attitudes Toward Older Individuals. *International Journal of Aging and Human Development*, 55(4), 341-66.

Kivett, V. (1993). Racial Comparison of the Grandmother Role: Implications for Strengthening the Family Support System of Older Black Women. *Family Relations*, 42(2), 165-72.

Kuehne, V. S. (1992). Older Adults in Intergenerational Programs: What Are Their Experiences Really Like? *Activities, Adaptation & Aging*, 16(4), 49-67.

Leon, A. & Leon, F. (1992). Intergenerational Programs for Young Children: Organizational Procedures. *Day Care and Early Education*, 19(3), 9-13.

Margoles, B. (1990). Rehema's Journey: A Visit in Tanzania. New York: Scholastic, Inc.

McGowen, M. R., Ladd, L., & Strom, R. D. (2006). On-Line Assessment of Grandmother Experience in Raising Grandchildren. *Educational Gerontology,* 32(8), 669-84.

Middlecamp, M. & Gross, D. (2010). Intergenerational Daycare and Preschoolers' Attitudes About Aging, *Educational Gerontology*, 28(4), 271-278.

Pantagraph (Illinois, June 22, 1998). Older People Taking Role in Raising Children.

Scherman, A. Efthimiadis, M. Gardner, J. E. & McLean, H. M. (1998). The Role of Panamanian Grandmothers in Family Systems that Include Grandchildren with Disabilities. *Educational Gerontology*, 24, pgs. 233-46.

Pak, Hwa-Ok (2005). Grandmothers Raising Grandchildren: Family Well-being and Economic Assistance. *Focus*, 24(1), 19-27.

Scherman, A., Efthimiadis, M., Gardner, J. E., & McLean, H. (1998). The Role of Panamanian Grandmothers in Family Systems That Include Grandchildren With Disabilities. *Educational Gerontology*, 24, 233-46.

Sheehan, R. (1978/. Young Children's Contact with the Elderly. *Journal of Gerontology*, 33(4), 567-574

Smith, A.B., Dannison, L., & Vach-Hasse (1998). When "Grandma" Is "Mom". *Childhood Education* 75(1).

Smith, A. (1999). Intergenerational Kinship "Parenting".Inquiry: *Research Scholarship & Creative Activity at the University of South Florida*, 2(1), 5.

Strom, R. & Strom, S. (1995). Intergenerational Learning: Grandparents in the Schools. *Educational Gerontology*, 21, 321-35

Woods, R. D. (1996). Grandmother Roles.: A Cross Cultural View. *Journal of Instructional Psychology*, 23, pgs. 286-92.

Printed in Dunstable, United Kingdom

67314733R00057